I CAN READ ABOUT
ESKIMOS

Written by Ellen Schultz
Illustrated by Herb Mott

Troll Associates

Far, far away in a region known as the Arctic,
the cold wind blows and the snow covers
the ground most of the year.

It is here that a strong and friendly group of people called Eskimos came to live many thousands of years ago. It is believed that they traveled across a land bridge from Siberia to Alaska. Most Eskimos settled in Alaska. Others journeyed on to northern Canada and Greenland.

They liked to call themselves Inuit— a special word meaning "the people."

The Eskimos learned to live on a land covered with ice and snow. It took much hard work just to survive.

They settled near the sea. There they caught fish and hunted seals, whales, and polar bears. They also hunted land animals called caribou, a kind of reindeer.

This is a tale of long ago...

Nanluk and his sister Sharni live with their mother and father in the Arctic, where winter lasts more than six months a year.

The first snow of winter is falling.
It is time for Nanluk and his family to build
a temporary winter snowhouse, or igloo. The
Eskimo word for any kind of house
is *igloo*.

Nanluk's father uses his bone snow knife to cut hard blocks of snow. The blocks are about 3 feet long. Together they stack row after row of blocks in a circle. Each row slants a little more inward until the blocks form a dome-shaped house. The cracks are packed with snow to keep the cold out. It always surprises Nanluk that they can finish their new igloo in only three or four hours.

Sharni and her mother help dig out the tunnel entrance to their igloo. Inside, they pack snow to make a platform above the floor. Then they put soft, warm animal skins across the top. This is the bed the family will sleep on.

Then they hang their soapstone pots on the walls and set aside a storage space for meats and family belongings.

Tonight Nanluk and his father must get lots of rest. Tomorrow they will leave to go hunting. The hunt for food is very important.

They must go early in the winter, when there is enough daylight. For several weeks in winter, the sun does not rise at all. Then there is darkness.

It is just the opposite in the summer, when the sun shines night and day for several weeks.

In the morning, they prepare the large sled and hitch the dog team in front. Sharni and her mother set out clothing and food for them. They will be gone many nights.

Father yells to the dogs, and they are off!

Along the way, they see a huge white polar bear, an Arctic fox, several Arctic hares, and a snowy owl. All these animals have adapted to their snowy surroundings by growing coats of white fur or feathers. This helps the animals blend into their surroundings and hide from their enemies.

The sled heads toward the sea.
It is here that they will hunt for seals
and fish. The ice is very thick,
but they know just what to do.

A seal is under the ice.
Seals make breathing holes in the ice. Nanluk and
his father wait by these holes to listen and watch.
They must be very patient. Finally, a seal pokes
its head near a hole for air.

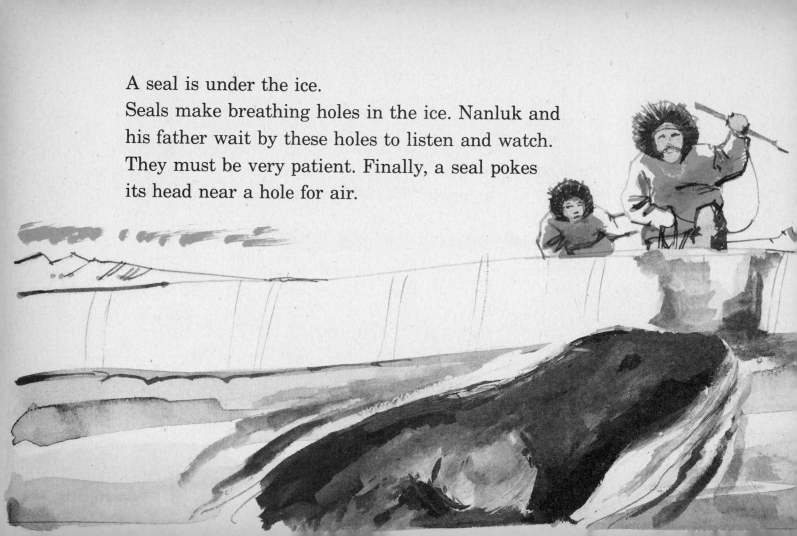

Quickly, Nanluk's father uses his harpoon and catches the seal. Nanluk also helps catch food by spearing small fish as they swim near a hole in the ice.

In the spring, the hunting is different. During the warmer months, the seals climb up onto the ice to sleep. Then Nanluk's father must sneak up on them very quietly.

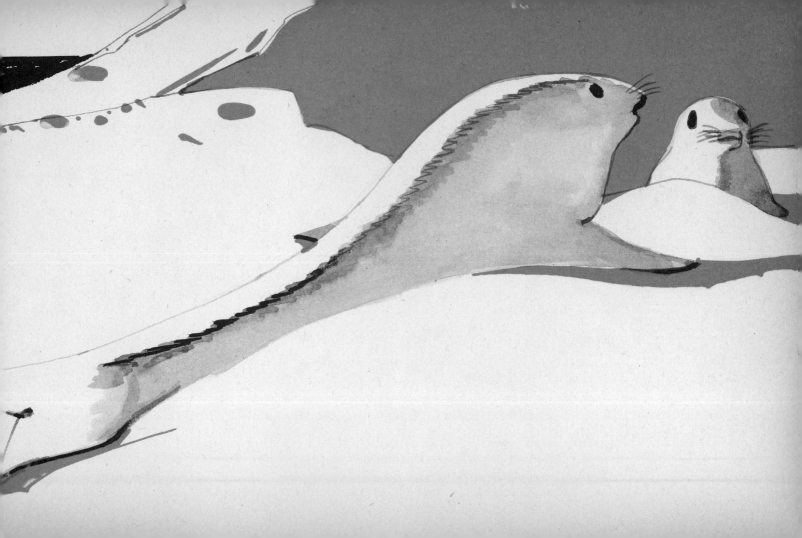

After many days, they have caught enough food to last
most of the winter. Now they start homeward again.

Sharni and her mother
make great use of the
seals. They scrape
off the thick skins.
Sometimes they chew
them to soften them.
The skins will be used
for clothing and
blankets, hand-sewn
parkas, even warm
boots. The blubber, or
fat, is used to make oil
for lamps. No part of
the animal is wasted.

Tonight there will be a feast. There will be raw seal meat, hot seal soup, and plenty of tea. How good it will be. The rest of the meat will be frozen and stored for future use.

Sometimes the cold wind and blowing snow
keep everyone indoors for days at a time.
But no one minds. Everyone takes great
joy in being together as a family. The
children play games and tell stories.
They have happy times in their snug home.

Nanluk and his father spend many evenings enjoying tug-of-war and other feats of strength.

Sharni and her mother decorate clothing with
beads and fur, or make special toys out of bone.

The days and long winter nights pass quickly.
Nanluk and Sharni wait for the arrival of spring and summer.
The warmer weather will not last very long. They must
make the most of every moment.

Summer means that Nanluk and his family will be leaving the snowhouse and moving into a land tent. The tent is made of deerskins and sealskins, saved from the year before.

The snow melts. The sun shines brightly.
Soon, there are colorful wild flowers, mosses,
and shrubs, even a few small trees.

Now the children spend all their time outdoors. Sharni loves to gather the beautiful flowers and bring them home.

The days become longer and longer. For a few weeks the sun does not set at all. This is why the Arctic is sometimes called the Land of the Midnight Sun.

During the summer, Nanluk and his father
go hunting for caribou. They hunt with spears
or with bows and arrows. The skins
are saved for the cold winter
months ahead and for next
summer's tent.

Gradually, the thick ice on the sea begins to crack and break up. Nanluk's father is building a boat that looks like a canoe. It is called a kayak. It is made with a wooden frame and covered with deerskin or sealskin. Kayaks are big enough to carry only one or two people, but they are an important method of transportation.

When they go hunting for whales or walruses in the sea,
Nanluk and his father use a larger, open boat called
an umiak.

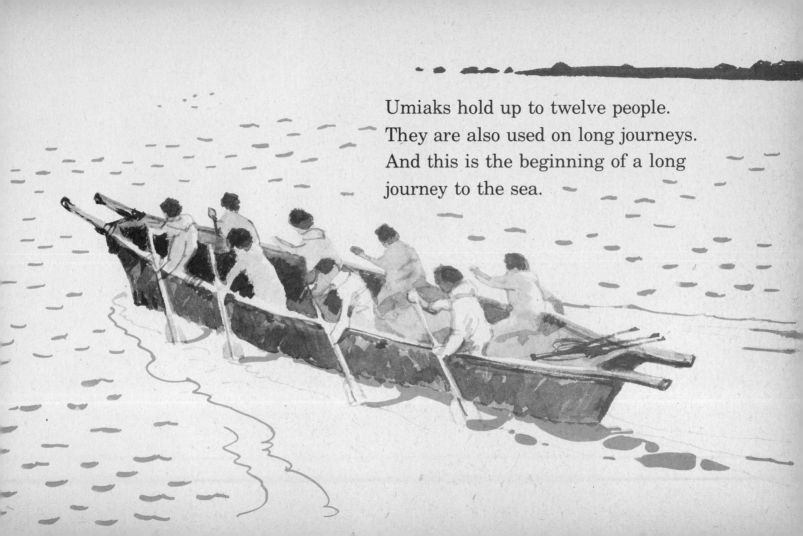

Umiaks hold up to twelve people.
They are also used on long journeys.
And this is the beginning of a long
journey to the sea.

Life has changed since Nanluk and Sharni were children.
That was life long ago ... And new things are happening.

Now Eskimos live in modern houses and shop at modern stores.
Eskimo children attend public schools.

And when the children
are out of school there
is always time for fun.

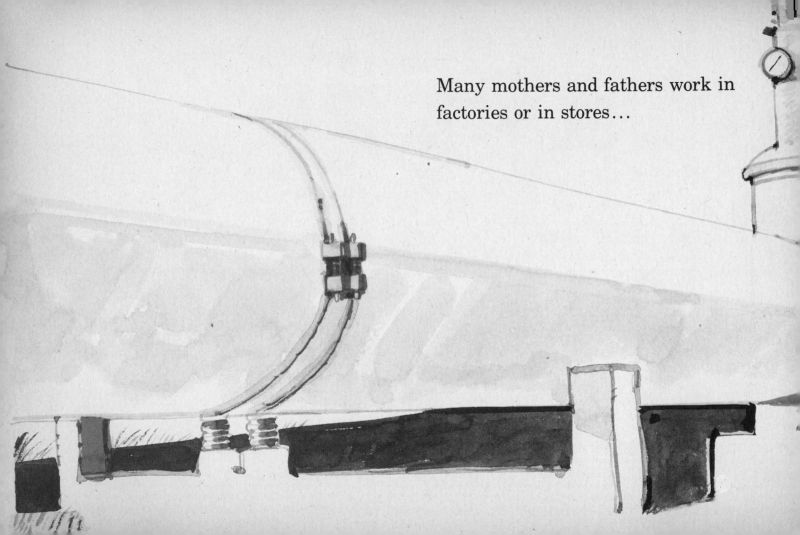

Many mothers and fathers work in
factories or in stores...

...or in big oil refineries.

And Eskimos have learned the new ways...
but they are still proud of the old traditions.